THE
Sight words
COLORING BOOK

THE Sight Words COLORING BOOK

A Fun Way to Teach Your Kid How to Read & Recognize Power Words

Martina Goulart

FOR YOUNG READERS

Racehorse for Young Readers books may be purchased in bulk at special discounts for sales promotion, corporate gifts, fund-raising, or educational purposes. Special editions can also be created to specifications. For details, contact the Special Sales Department, Skyhorse Publishing, 307 West 36th Street, 11th Floor, New York, NY 10018 or info@skyhorsepublishing.com.

Racehorse for Young Readers™ is a pending trademark of Skyhorse Publishing, Inc.®, a Delaware corporation.

Visit our website at www.skyhorsepublishing.com.

10 9 8 7 6 5 4 3

Cover design by Mona Lin
Text and illustrations by Martina Goulart

Print ISBN: 978-1-63158-333-9

Printed in China

CONTENTS

100 High-Frequency and Sight Words Collection for Children

THE Sight words COLORING BOOK

Color the word of the page you have finished.

Word of the page is _____ . I found it _____ times.

Color the picture.

Think of whole sentences or a story using the word of the page. Tell it to someone.

Word of the page is _____ . I found it _____ times.

Color the picture.

Think of whole sentences or a story using the word of the page. Tell it to someone.

2

Word of the page is _____ . I found it _____ times.

Color the picture.
Think of whole sentences or a story using the word of the page. Tell it to someone.

Word of the page is _____ . I found it _____ times.

Color the picture.

Think of whole sentences or a story using the word of the page. Tell it to someone.

Word of the page is _____ . I found it _____ times.

Color the picture.

Think of whole sentences or a story using the word of the page. Tell it to someone.

Word of the page is _____ . I found it _____ times.

Color the picture.
Think of whole sentences or a story using the word of the page. Tell it to someone.

6

Word of the page is _____ .   I found it _____ times.

Color the picture.

Think of whole sentences or a story using the word of the page. Tell it to someone.

Word of the page is _____ . I found it _____ times.

Color the picture.

Think of whole sentences or a story using the word of the page. Tell it to someone.

Word of the page is _____ . I found it _____ times.

Color the picture.

Think of whole sentences or a story using the word of the page. Tell it to someone.

Word of the page is _____ . I found it _____ times.

Color the picture.

Think of whole sentences or a story using the word of the page. Tell it to someone.

Word of the page is _____ . I found it _____ times.

Color the picture.

Think of whole sentences or a story using the word of the page. Tell it to someone.

Word of the page is _____ . I found it _____ times.

Color the picture.
Think of whole sentences or a story using the word of the page. Tell it to someone.

Word of the page is _____ .   I found it _____ times.

Color the picture.

Think of whole sentences or a story using the word of the page. Tell it to someone.

Word of the page is _____ . I found it _____ times.

Color the picture.

Think of whole sentences or a story using the word of the page. Tell it to someone.

Word of the page is _____ . I found it _____ times.

Color the picture.

Think of whole sentences or a story using the word of the page. Tell it to someone. 15

Word of the page is _____ . I found it _____ times.

Color the picture.

Think of whole sentences or a story using the word of the page. Tell it to someone.

Word of the page is _____ . I found it _____ times.

Color the picture.

Think of whole sentences or a story using the word of the page. Tell it to someone.

Word of the page is _____ .   I found it _____ times.

Color the picture.
Think of whole sentences or a story using the word of the page. Tell it to someone.   18

Word of the page is _____ . I found it _____ times.

Color the picture.
Think of whole sentences or a story using the word of the page. Tell it to someone.   19

Word of the page is _____ . I found it _____ times.

Color the picture.

Think of whole sentences or a story using the word of the page. Tell it to someone. 20

Word of the page is _____ . I found it _____ times.

Color the picture.

Think of whole sentences or a story using the word of the page. Tell it to someone.

Word of the page is _____ .   I found it _____ times.

Color the picture.
Think of whole sentences or a story using the word of the page. Tell it to someone.   22

Word of the page is _____ . I found it _____ times.

do DO do DO do DO do DO do DO do DO do

Color the picture.

Think of whole sentences or a story using the word of the page. Tell it to someone.

23

Word of the page is _____ . I found it _____ times.

Color the picture.

Think of whole sentences or a story using the word of the page. Tell it to someone.

Word of the page is _____ . I found it _____ times.

Color the picture.

Think of whole sentences or a story using the word of the page. Tell it to someone.   25

Word of the page is _____ . I found it _____ times.

Color the picture.
Think of whole sentences or a story using the word of the page. Tell it to someone. 26

Word of the page is _____ . I found it _____ times.

Color the picture.

Think of whole sentences or a story using the word of the page. Tell it to someone.

_____   _____

-    - - - - - - - - - -

Word of the page is _____ .   I found it _____ times.

Color the picture.

Think of whole sentences or a story using the word of the page. Tell it to someone.   28

Word of the page is _____ . I found it _____ times.

Color the picture.
Think of whole sentences or a story using the word of the page. Tell it to someone. 29

Word of the page is _____ . I found it _____ times.

Color the picture.

Think of whole sentences or a story using the word of the page. Tell it to someone.   30

Word of the page is _____ . I found it _____ times.

Color the picture.
Think of whole sentences or a story using the word of the page. Tell it to someone.   31

Word of the page is _____ . I found it _____ times.

Color the picture.

Think of whole sentences or a story using the word of the page. Tell it to someone.

Word of the page is _____ . I found it _____ times.

Color the picture.
Think of whole sentences or a story using the word of the page. Tell it to someone.

Word of the page is _____ . I found it _____ times.

Color the picture.
Think of whole sentences or a story using the word of the page. Tell it to someone. 34

Word of the page is _____ .   I found it _____ times.

Color the picture.
Think of whole sentences or a story using the word of the page. Tell it to someone.

Word of the page is _____ . I found it _____ times.

Color the picture.

Think of whole sentences or a story using the word of the page. Tell it to someone.   36

Word of the page is _____ . I found it _____ times.

Color the picture.

Think of whole sentences or a story using the word of the page. Tell it to someone.

Word of the page is _____ . I found it _____ times.

Color the picture.
Think of whole sentences or a story using the word of the page. Tell it to someone.

Word of the page is _____ .   I found it _____ times.

Color the picture.

Think of whole sentences or a story using the word of the page. Tell it to someone.

Word of the page is _____ .   I found it _____ times.

Color the picture.
Think of whole sentences or a story using the word of the page. Tell it to someone.   40

Word of the page is _____ . I found it _____ times.

Color the picture.

Think of whole sentences or a story using the word of the page. Tell it to someone.

41

Word of the page is _____ . I found it _____ times.

Color the picture.
Think of whole sentences or a story using the word of the page. Tell it to someone.

Word of the page is _____ . I found it _____ times.

Color the picture.

Think of whole sentences or a story using the word of the page. Tell it to someone.

Word of the page is _____ . I found it _____ times.

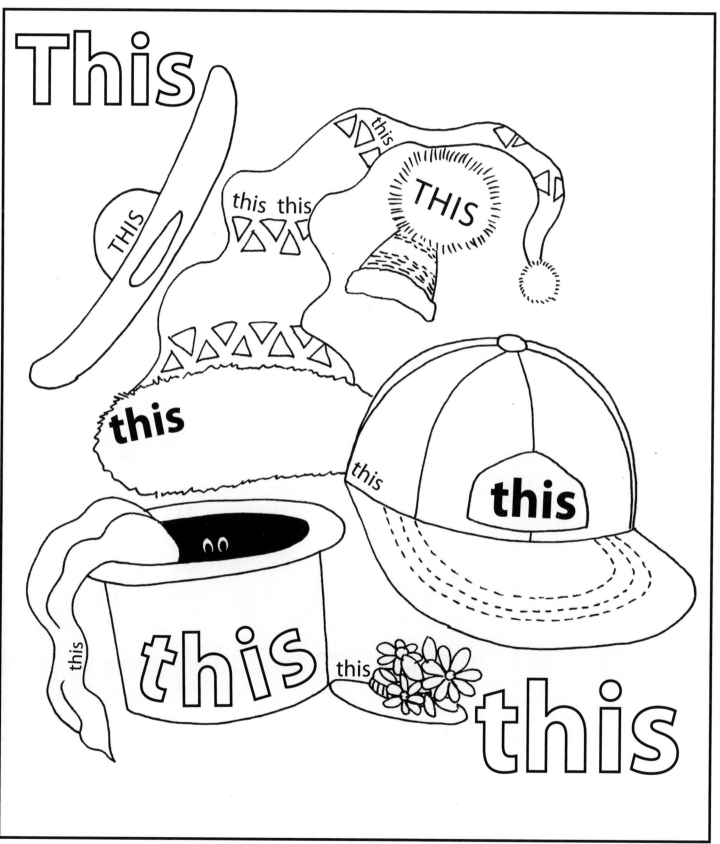

Color the picture.

Think of whole sentences or a story using the word of the page. Tell it to someone.

Word of the page is _____ . I found it _____ times.

Color the picture.

Think of whole sentences or a story using the word of the page. Tell it to someone.

45

Word of the page is _____ .   I found it _____ times.

Color the picture.

Think of whole sentences or a story using the word of the page. Tell it to someone.

Word of the page is _____ .   I found it _____ times.

Color the picture.

Think of whole sentences or a story using the word of the page. Tell it to someone.   47

Word of the page is _____ . I found it _____ times.

Color the picture.
Think of whole sentences or a story using the word of the page. Tell it to someone.

Word of the page is _____ . I found it _____ times.

Color the picture.

Think of whole sentences or a story using the word of the page. Tell it to someone.   49

Word of the page is _____ . I found it _____ times.

Color the picture.
Think of whole sentences or a story using the word of the page. Tell it to someone.

Word of the page is _____ . I found it _____ times.

Color the picture.
Think of whole sentences or a story using the word of the page. Tell it to someone.

Word of the page is _____ . I found it _____ times.

Color the picture.

Think of whole sentences or a story using the word of the page. Tell it to someone.

Word of the page is _____ . I found it _____ times.

Color the picture.

Think of whole sentences or a story using the word of the page. Tell it to someone. 53

Word of the page is _____ . I found it _____ times.

Color the picture.
Think of whole sentences or a story using the word of the page. Tell it to someone.

Word of the page is _____ . I found it _____ times.

Color the picture.

Think of whole sentences or a story using the word of the page. Tell it to someone.   55

Word of the page is _____ .   I found it _____ times.

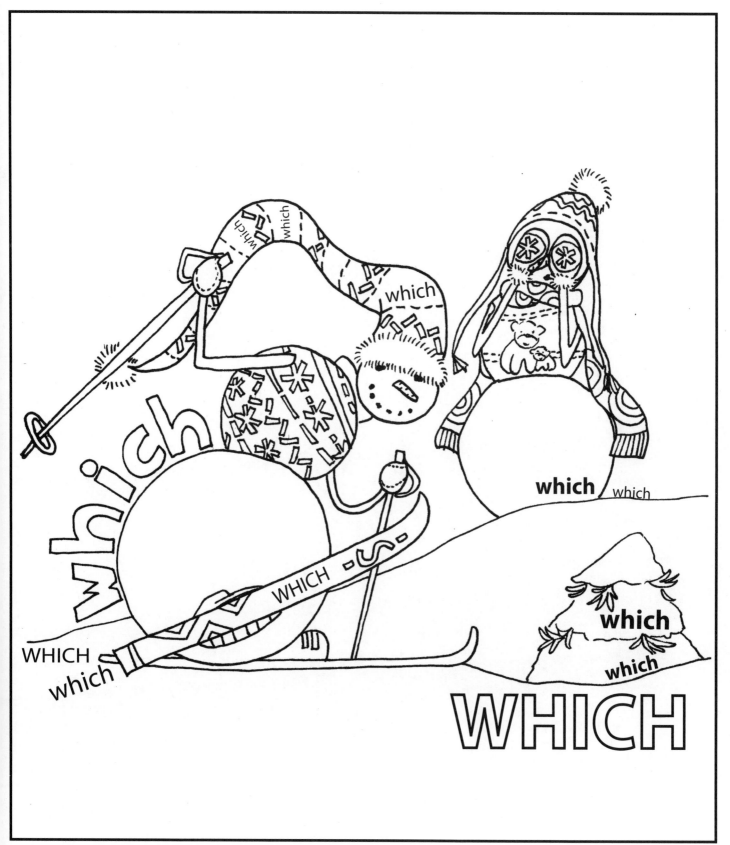

Color the picture.

Think of whole sentences or a story using the word of the page. Tell it to someone.

Word of the page is _____ .   I found it _____ times.

Color the picture.

Think of whole sentences or a story using the word of the page. Tell it to someone.

Word of the page is _____ . I found it _____ times.

Color the picture.
Think of whole sentences or a story using the word of the page. Tell it to someone.

Word of the page is _____ . I found it _____ times.

Color the picture.
Think of whole sentences or a story using the word of the page. Tell it to someone.

Word of the page is _____ . I found it _____ times.

Color the picture.
Think of whole sentences or a story using the word of the page. Tell it to someone.

Word of the page is _____ . I found it _____ times.

Color the picture.
Think of whole sentences or a story using the word of the page. Tell it to someone.

Word of the page is _____ . I found it _____ times.

Color the picture.
Think of whole sentences or a story using the word of the page. Tell it to someone.

Word of the page is _____ .   I found it _____ times.

Color the picture.

Think of whole sentences or a story using the word of the page. Tell it to someone.   63

Word of the page is _____ . I found it _____ times.

Color the picture.

Think of whole sentences or a story using the word of the page. Tell it to someone.

Word of the page is _____ .   I found it _____ times.

Color the picture.

Think of whole sentences or a story using the word of the page. Tell it to someone.

Word of the page is _____ . I found it _____ times.

Color the picture.

Think of whole sentences or a story using the word of the page. Tell it to someone.

Word of the page is _____ . I found it _____ times.

Color the picture.

Think of whole sentences or a story using the word of the page. Tell it to someone.

Word of the page is _____ . I found it _____ times.

Color the picture.

Think of whole sentences or a story using the word of the page. Tell it to someone.

68

Word of the page is _____ . I found it _____ times.

Color the picture.

Think of whole sentences or a story using the word of the page. Tell it to someone.

Word of the page is _____ . I found it _____ times.

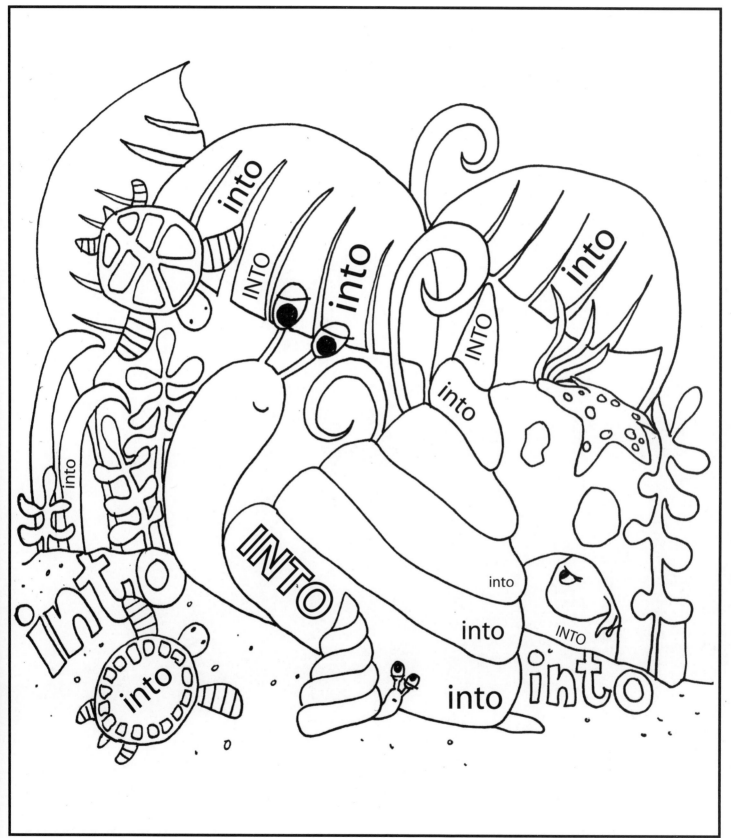

Color the picture.

Think of whole sentences or a story using the word of the page. Tell it to someone.   70

Word of the page is _____ .   I found it _____ times.

Color the picture.

Think of whole sentences or a story using the word of the page. Tell it to someone.   71

Word of the page is _____ . I found it _____ times.

Color the picture.

Think of whole sentences or a story using the word of the page. Tell it to someone.

Word of the page is _____ . I found it _____ times.

Color the picture.

Think of whole sentences or a story using the word of the page. Tell it to someone.

Word of the page is _____ . I found it _____ times.

Color the picture.

Think of whole sentences or a story using the word of the page. Tell it to someone.

Word of the page is _____ . I found it _____ times.

Color the picture.

Think of whole sentences or a story using the word of the page. Tell it to someone.

Word of the page is _____ . I found it _____ times.

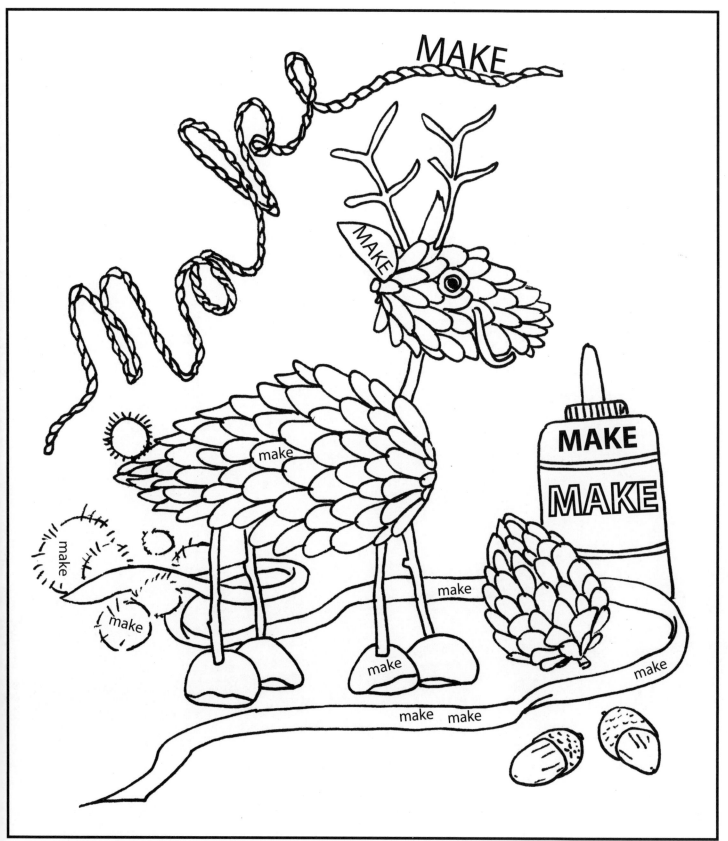

Color the picture.

Think of whole sentences or a story using the word of the page. Tell it to someone.

Word of the page is _____.   I found it _____ times.

Color the picture.

Think of whole sentences or a story using the word of the page. Tell it to someone.

Word of the page is _____ .   I found it _____ times.

Color the picture.

Think of whole sentences or a story using the word of the page. Tell it to someone.   78

Word of the page is _____ .   I found it _____ times.

Color the picture.

Think of whole sentences or a story using the word of the page. Tell it to someone.

Word of the page is _____ . I found it _____ times.

Color the picture.

Think of whole sentences or a story using the word of the page. Tell it to someone.

Word of the page is _____ . I found it _____ times.

Color the picture.

Think of whole sentences or a story using the word of the page. Tell it to someone.

Word of the page is _____ .   I found it _____ times.

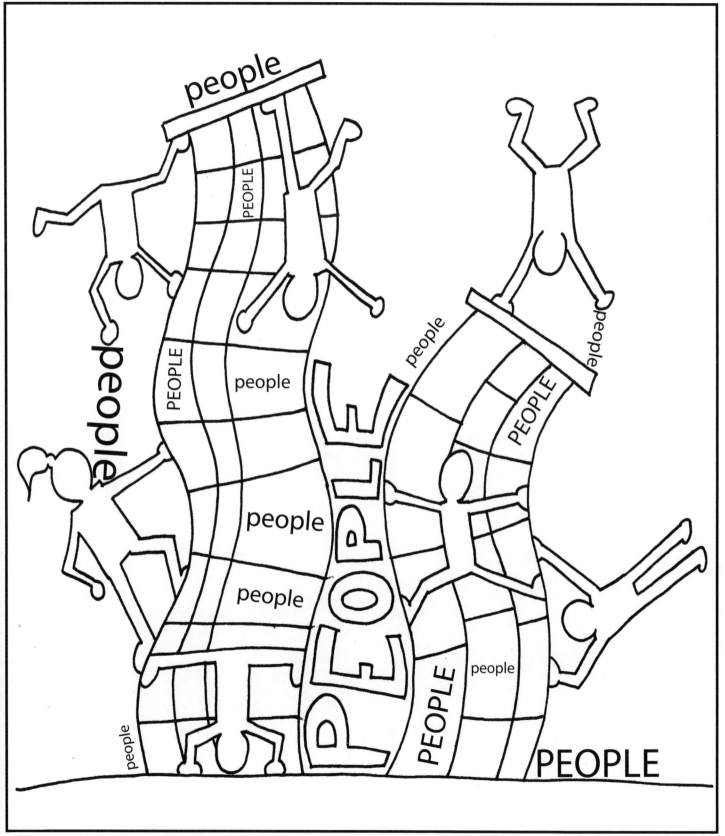

Color the picture.
Think of whole sentences or a story using the word of the page. Tell it to someone.   82

Word of the page is _____ . I found it _____ times.

OVER   OVER   OVER   OVER

Color the picture.

Think of whole sentences or a story using the word of the page. Tell it to someone.

Word of the page is _____ . I found it _____ times.

Color the picture.

Think of whole sentences or a story using the word of the page. Tell it to someone.

Word of the page is _____ . I found it _____ times.

Color the picture.

Think of whole sentences or a story using the word of the page. Tell it to someone.

Word of the page is _____ . I found it _____ times.

Color the picture.
Think of whole sentences or a story using the word of the page. Tell it to someone.

Word of the page is _____ . I found it _____ times.

Color the picture.

Think of whole sentences or a story using the word of the page. Tell it to someone.

Word of the page is _____ . I found it _____ times.

Color the picture.

Think of whole sentences or a story using the word of the page. Tell it to someone.

Word of the page is _____ .   I found it _____ times.

Color the picture.

Think of whole sentences or a story using the word of the page. Tell it to someone.   89

Word of the page is _____ .   I found it _____ times.

Color the picture.
Think of whole sentences or a story using the word of the page. Tell it to someone.

Word of the page is _____ .　I found it _____ times.

Color the picture.
Think of whole sentences or a story using the word of the page. Tell it to someone.

Word of the page is _____ . I found it _____ times.

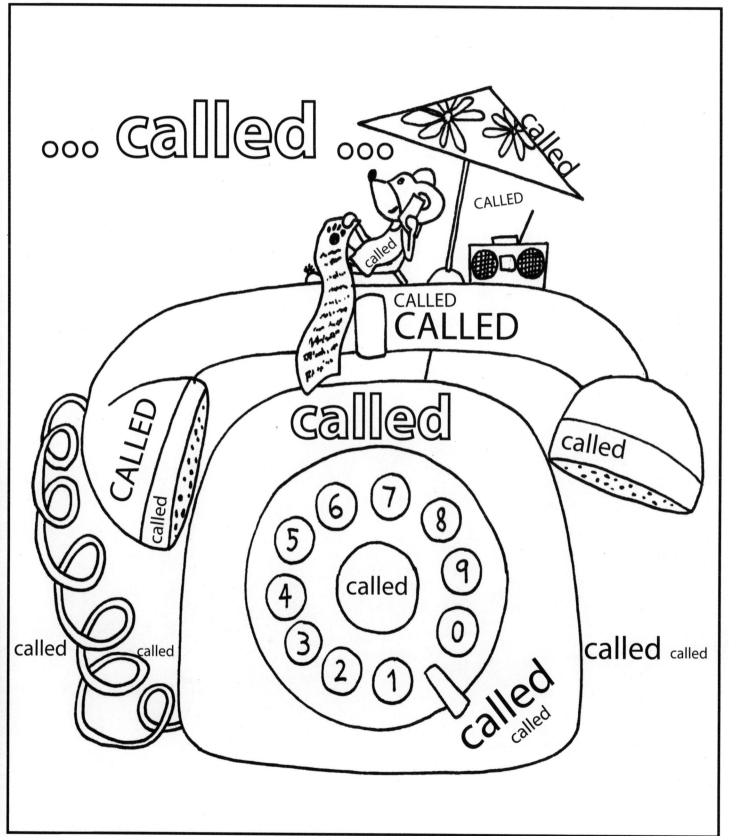

Color the picture.

Think of whole sentences or a story using the word of the page. Tell it to someone.

Word of the page is _____ . I found it _____ times.

Color the picture.

Think of whole sentences or a story using the word of the page. Tell it to someone.

Word of the page is _____ .   I found it _____ times.

Color the picture.

Think of whole sentences or a story using the word of the page. Tell it to someone.

Word of the page is _____ . I found it _____ times.

Color the picture.

Think of whole sentences or a story using the word of the page. Tell it to someone.

Word of the page is _____ . I found it _____ times.

Color the picture.

Think of whole sentences or a story using the word of the page. Tell it to someone.

Word of the page is _____ . I found it _____ times.

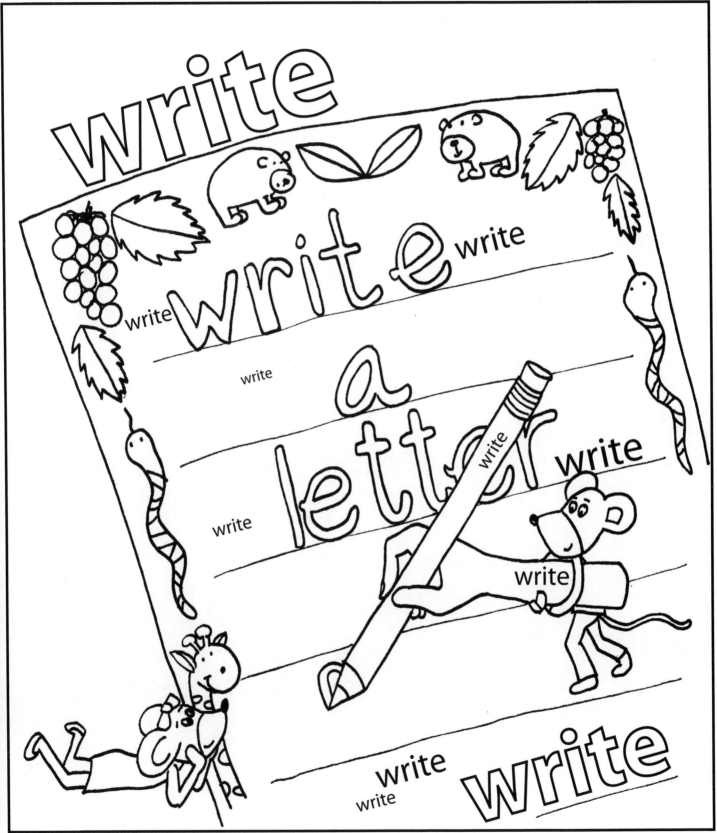

Color the picture.
Think of whole sentences or a story using the word of the page. Tell it to someone.   97

Word of the page is _____ .   I found it _____ times.

Color the picture.

Think of whole sentences or a story using the word of the page. Tell it to someone.

Word of the page is _____ .   I found it _____ times.

Color the picture.
Think of whole sentences or a story using the word of the page. Tell it to someone.

Word of the page is _____ . I found it _____ times.

Color the picture.

Think of whole sentences or a story using the word of the page. Tell it to someone.